# Moments

## For the

## Spiritually Aware

## Parent

Christina Fletcher

# Introduction

I'm so excited about creating this book, *Moments for the Spiritually Aware Parent*. Over the last year, this book has been an amazing journey of creation, not only by the thoughts and words, not only through the process of pen to paper, rather it has been the defining of what Spiritually Aware Parenting, and Spiritually Aware living, is all about.

This book contains a compilation of the statuses and updates I have written for my Spiritually Aware Parenting Facebook page, since its birth in March 2011. I have been thrilled with the heart warming response to my daily words and with people's appreciation for the small passages that have often proved challenging to keep within the 420 character limit. Over this past year, my family and I have experienced many transitions and the writing of these short paragraphs has provided me with the groundedness and connection that I needed to remain spiritually aware myself.

Writing provides me with connection. The words form themselves out of nowhere and I often find my pen moving over an empty page without even knowing what I will write.

Each of these paragraphs you find on the following pages, have been inspired from day to day living with my amazing children. We all have a balance of good and bad days, the bad days providing the contrast needed to grow and expand, knowing what we don't want so we know what we do. These short blurbs have been my process of finding the awareness, the perspective, of the spiritually aware parent in all those moments and to appreciate the days that are filled with joy and awe inspiring laughter, and the ones that are not, alike.

I hope you enjoy this collection. It is designed to be flicked through, that your eyes may land on just the words you need to hear, although it can also be read in order, daily or whenever your own inspiration strikes.

And so a cycle has been created. In writing these passages Spiritually Aware Parenting has defined itself, and in defining itself, these words have been written. I have met amazing people through this, and I appreciate them all daily. I have been enlightening, encouraged, and inspired by my Facebook followers and from what I gather, have often done the same for them. I am eager for the adventure that lies ahead as we continue to co-create together.

I dedicate this book to my husband, who lifts me up to new heights, inspires me, lights up my world (sorts out my artwork and suggested I do it in the first place!) and makes it so easy to appreciate the life we have together, also to our children, Abigail, Giana and Frederick, who inspire me constantly and have truly helped Spiritually Aware Parenting become what it has become, and to all of my Facebook followers. You are a wonderful community, and it's lovely to produce this book amongst like minded friends.

Be Well, Happy and Thrive

vi

Our children chose us for everything we really are. Therefore, we do them no good by denying ourselves *our own* joys and passions.

Often, parenting can be seen as a time of sacrifice of our dreams. But when we don't jive ourselves, we can't be spiritually present for our children.

We also can't give them the full experience of ourselves, which is why they chose us in the first place.

By looking for thoughts that make you feel better, you open yourself to solutions rather then focusing on the problems. We can't deny problems, only use them as launching pads for the next solution.

Breathe and relax. Find a thought that makes you feel better and practice it. As it builds more thoughts will come until you find a place where you are jiving again. When you return your thoughts to the problem, you will find solutions will flow in.

This moment in time,
*NOW,* is what matters.
However easy it is to put our attention on
tomorrow and what it will bring or on the
past and what occurred, it is in this Now
that living takes place.
Savour it, make it an amazing moment,
make it feel good, let it wash over you and
in doing so watch each following moment
get better and better.

Everything that has gone before has brought us to the place and perspective of where we stand today. With it behind us, we can offer our children and all of those around us a newer, fuller version of us. Appreciate the past, as it has made you who you are, and live today as everything you really are.

We aren't in a competition, and we have nothing to prove. We can't get it wrong and never get it done, and each time something we do feels off, it just makes what feels right clearer. Therefore, don't worry if you have a bad moment. Choose to feel better, practice it, feel the relief, grow, expand.

What an example for our children: to *feel* the offness and control our thoughts to feel good again.

Proof of what we believe will always present itself. Therefore, expect the best and the universe will pull out all the stops to match the feeling of your expectation.

Often, our children's off behaviour is what we come to expect. Therefore, it's all we see even when they are behaving as Who They Really Are.
If we look only for  the best in our children, without criticism or judgement they will rise to the occasion and the best is all we will be able to see.

Feeling overwhelmed and slightly frustrated?
Does everything seem to be going wrong?

Find the time to play with your children. Stop the tangled mess and the pushing against what you really want, get on the floor and play.
Rather then using our children as an excuse to feel negative emotion, when we shift gears, play and have fun, we create an excuse to feel good anyway and our children and us reap the benefits.

when our children offer us "problem" behaviour, it's a question of helping them connect rather than teaching them right or wrong.

They feel the offness of what doesn't make them feel good. Therefore, change the energy of the moment. Make them laugh, distract, refocus on something else and change how the moment feels. They'll usually shift with you and you won't have to join them in negative space by getting mad.

It takes just a split second to feel better.

Even when life is at its craziness, and when overwhelment is right around the corner, when we take a breath and take a step back from what seems so frantic, settling into a sense of self and connection, when we look around ourselves again, our perception will have changed.

Take the moment to feel good, even just think the thought to refocus, and then let life shift.

Our children burble, dance and play with excitement when they are connected. If we're feeling off, their joy of connection can add to our offness as we shift from seeing their jiving to seeing them as not listening, their dancing as not sitting still, their play as lack of focus.

When we remind ourselves that they are jiving and we are the ones feeling Off, we allow their connection to inspire our own.

Other people's opinions can really throw all of us out of a feel good place. From other parents sharing their perspectives, to a little child feeling they have to act cute in order to make others happy, we all feel the effects of the social mirror.

However it is by looking at ourselves through our inner reflection, that we can return to feeling whole again and offer the world the truest likeness of ourselves.

*Fear looks at the worst case scenario.*

*Love looks at the best.*

*Fear lives in the future.*

*Love lives in the Now.*

*Fear disguises itself as worry, concern, anxiety, stress and frustration.*

*Love needs no disguises, as it always comes from everything We Really Are.*

It's so important to be honest with how we feel. If we try to convince ourselves of feeling different then we do, we prevent ourselves from ever actually, truly feeling better. When we claim how we feel we can then appreciate, love, change perspective, dream and raise ourselves up to feeling better.

What a tool for our children to witness, to be truly aware and in control of our emotional systems.

It is a common misunderstanding to view children as just that "children". We are often given generalized suggestions of what "children" need or how *they* feel.

But in truth, each child is different and requires different things and feels uniquely to themselves, just as we all do. It is by understanding a child in their uniqueness, even from within the womb, that we can connect to them and offer them what we feel is the right at the time.

we all have different ways of thinking.

We each come here to observe and make decisions of preference, so it would be futile to believe we all think the same.

Even our children can see the world different than us. Therefore, rather than criticize difference, if we try to see through other people's eyes and perception, we release ourselves from the restraint of seclusion and enter a place where we can truly learn from others.

Appreciation is a powerful thing.
From any position we can feel better by
simply appreciating something or
someone in our lives.

It is a powerful thing to pass this ability on
to our children. To be able to appreciate
the little things in life, *water, the pillow on our
bed, the ability to breathe and relax, the sun, that
morning coffee.* By letting the feeling of
appreciation flow over us, we become
present and awake in our now, ready for
whatever life, and our children, have to
offer us.

when we radiate joy, our children will join in. When we ooze of stress, chances are our children will pick it up.

When we are honest about our own emotional states, then we own how we feel, and allow our children to be honest about their own.

Sometimes just stating the words "I'm feeling off today, I better work at feeling better," can help our children realize that how they feel can be up to them.

It feels good to feel good.

When facing the option of being mad or being sympathetic, feel good.

Give a hug rather than a shout, a deep breath rather than a frustrated shrug. Choose to see the best in your children, rather than the little things that annoy, see the beauty in the world rather than focus on the pain.

Feel Good, and find each day feel even better.

Be attentive and enjoy.

Source has infinite ways to create opportunity.

All you have to do is let it in.

There are days when everything goes wrong. Shoes are lost, you run late, hit traffic and spill on your only clean shirt.

The law of attraction brings the chain of events into your day. But it can also work in reverse, causing a series of good things to flow in. It's not good luck, it's a response to the feeling you are omitting.

Therefore, focus on the positive and feel good.

Have a day full of wellbeing.

From the moment of conception we have the opportunity to create a beautiful world for our children. Through being aware of how we feel, and how they do, and always reaching for the better feeling option, we can offer them all of who we are and sense what they need on a deeper level, offer them a launching place of connection and a chance to have well being as their default.

when our children are made aware of the law of attraction they can find evidence of it throughout their everyday life. Frustration breeds more frustration, sadness more sadness, joy more joy, laughter more laughter.

They will also understand how this works in the lives of those around them, and rather than get upset by others, see the connection between the thoughts others think and how it affects how they are.

when we try to control life, our focus becomes based in the future and we avoid things through fear.

When we focus on our joy of the moment, relaxing in feeling good NOW, we can trust the universe and await for joyful opportunities to appear.

When we allow the same for our children, and trust in their own Now, we offer them the same opportunities, and empower them to be Who They Really Are.

Let it all flow in.

It's being aware of the little joys that make life wonderful.

Appreciating those moments when you and your child share

a laugh,

a sparkle, a smile.

Those brilliant times, when you connect together, a spark is ignited. By focusing on those sparks, and carrying that feeling with you through out the day, you create opportunity to spark more. It's the difference between joyful moments and walking through the motions.

Each of us gets the urge to explore, and gain new vantage points.

Each baby will want to crawl, no matter how hard we want them in our arms, and each child will form their own questions and answers, no matter how hard we want them to agree with us.

Rather than resisting change within our children we can enjoy the now, and be eager for the new.

For our children understand the best is always yet to come.

Anything can affect how we feel: a song, a movie, a tv show, a game, even the conversations around us.

When our children are bombarded with negative feelings, even through media, it is asking too much of them to find a better feeling place outside of that. Therefore, create a beautiful world for children, with feeling good things in it. They will feel the offness of the other, and become aware of the difference.

seize the moment, not just the day.

Sometimes we can be lost in our own thoughts and then our children will ask for a hug, a story, or even a glass of water. By seizing that moment, soaking up the look in our child's eyes, we connect. As we appreciate it we reactivate our day, and when we return to what we were doing we find ourselves happier and tapped back in to the flow of wellbeing.

Every aspect of our babies' lives can be approached by being spiritually aware.

Often we are faced with decisions, big or small, and when we find a quiet spot within and connect to everything we really are, one option will always feel better then the other. One will bring relief while the other feels off.
By going with the one that brings relief you will be following your own inner truth.

Days can often turn into a steady flow of "To do's" and "have to's" But by feeling overwhelmed we create a frustrating experience for both us and our children.

We have to allow ourselves a bit of
*relief.*
Take time to play, to laugh and connect with your child. You will feel better, your child will too and thru the Law of Attraction your lists will get done with the same relieving sense of joy.

Being spiritually aware doesn't mean we have to be connected all the time.

The times of off-ness is a time of new creation, as then we ask for better, while when we are "on" we ride the wave of what we created. Therefore being aware just means observe how you feel. When you feel off, appreciate the asking stage, and then work to feel better, which will connect you to your Source and everything you've asked for.

The golden rule of
*"treat people as you want to be treated"*,
is one of the strongest tools for being
spiritually aware.

It reminds us to act rather then react and
leads into the concept of
"you get what you give."
To pass this on to our children empowers
them to be the creator of their days and to
take control of their own perspective. It
also teaches consideration, which is the
basis of a happy home.

Often we can focus our attention onto our children's future with thoughts such as

"how will they turn out?!"

However when we relax and refocus on each moment, they become the stepping stones to the unseen goal.

We <u>can't</u> have a happy destination without a happy journey, there's no point trying.

Don't you love the chatter of a child's
imaginary game?
Children act from pure connection,
without social constraints or caring what
others think.

The imagination is something we
should never grow out of. It is from that
place where dreams are formed and happy
days created. We should all strive to have
our imaginary worlds as vivid in our
thoughts as our "real" ones.
Then the one will influence the other.

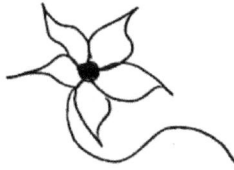

To feel good doesn't mean you do what you want, when you want, at the expense of others, including our children.

One can never truly feel good when others suffer. Rather, by using our thoughts to create that true good feeling place, we connect to the Source that we all are from.

The ways to help and care for others will then arise as inspired action.

Our own childhood can stir up a lot of emotions within us, and we often look back on it logically to judge *"I will do this"* or *"I won't do that"*.

However, when we look at our past through our own eyes as a child, the events that took place don't matter as much as how we felt then. We can then see and feel through our own child's perspective and can use that understanding to connect to our children on a deeper level.

Often our children will do things that
feel "off" to us.
This starts at an early age, as they start
to interpret the world around them. It is
important to remember that what feels
"off" to us, might feel "on" to them.
It is only through distraction and
offering them alternatives that we can
nurture different perspectives.

Demanding they be as we are, and like
what we like never gets us anywhere.

Sometimes it feels like we are always on call and that we never get a moment to sit and just *be* without someone calling our name.

Relax in all of this. It's in our thoughts that "*be-ing*" takes place, not specific times or places.

Therefore by changing our perspective by focusing on the positive and appreciating everything we can, we take part in our children's reality and "*be*" in our own at the same time.

Parenting provides us with so many opportunies to grow and define ourselves. Children ask us things we never thought of before, they offer problems that we need to feel a solution for, and they help us notice and appreciate so many wonderful things this world has to offer.

When we rise to the occasion and seize the moment, we in turn offer them the same opportunity:

We grow together.

*Take a step back and look into your inner mirror.*

*Do you feel like the person/parent you wish to be?*

*When you see your inner reflection, is there conflict between who you want to be and what you present?*

*Don't worry if there is, that's part of the process.*

*Dream of the higher version of yourself. Imagine it, feel it, be it.*

*Trust that with that bit of work, who you dream to be will shine through.*

Doesn't it change perspective on negative experiences to see them as signals from Source to change course via the law of attraction?

To see every bump, fall, accident or stressful moment as an indicator to shift how we feel?

So often these moments make us more upset, but if we use them as flashing lights infront of us, we can slow down, refocus, laugh, and change direction.

What a tool to pass on to our darlings.

Ask and it is given.

Whenever you feel that you aren't parenting as you wish, imagine how you would like it to feel and allow it to flow in. If you don't know how you wish it would be, than just offer the request for the opportunity to feel better, and trust for the moment to come.

Watch and wait, breathe and allow. What your children need from you will flow in, just at the right time. There's no reason to push...

just trust.

Perception is what shapes us and creates our days.

How we view the world is the basement for how things flow into our lives, whether we see it as a struggle or as based in wellbeing.

By helping our children find the positive, by focusing on wellbeing ourselves and by offering them options of different perceptions in various situations, we can keep them in their natural state of feeling good, and feel good ourselves.

when we are aware of how we feel, we can take shortcuts to feeling better.

If we're stressed or overwhelmed, we can shift our focus to something else, we can play with our children, hold our babies, cuddle them, kiss them.

We can choose to seize the moment and feel better, and then, when we look at what was stressful, we will find it will flow without aggravation letting life be the stressfree journey it was meant to be.

From infancy we reach for new experiences and then often feel disconnected when we get there. However, when we distract ourselves, shift focus from what feels off and trust that all is well, we slowly become accustomed to the new space.

Life is a steady flow of moving forward, focus on the wellbeing and adjust to the new perspective, relying on the Source that took you to new heights.

when dealing with more than one child in a family its important to keep a common balance.

Each child has their own connection to source, and will have their own off moments and connected ones. However, by finding your own connection first, and trusting that wellbeing flows, you can create a home where connection is natural and all members will tap into it.

Reach for joy, trust in wellbeing and all will thrive.

As tempting as it is to try to control our child's feeling space, in truth they are the only ones who can make themselves feel happiness at their core.

As parents we can only offer them opportunities to feel better and distractions to raise their emotional state, reminding them that it is natural for all of us to feel good and it's a process of moving through the off times not getting in the habit of them.

The word "don't" is easy to use day to day as an attempt to control circumstances. We imagine the worst that could happen, say "don't try it" and then attract the negative outcomes anyway.

Give the benefit of the doubt and enpower your children by allowing them to see where their choices take them, when no danger is present.

Be a "*do*" parent, not a "*don't*" one and your children will relax to rise to the occasion.

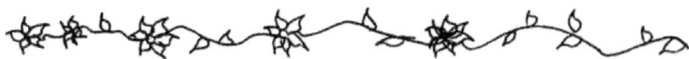

Our own chattering mind can drown out the voices of our children, who then feel unheard.

Become present in thought as well as body. Shift focus to what your children are saying, and if something else comes up that requires mind space, be honest with them.

Take the time to have a quiet moment before bed, centring thoughts and focusing yourself, which will set the new day up for joyous conversation.

Follow the ease and flow of it all.

Chose the peaceful path, the joyous road, and our children will respond to it.

Even if we wish they would stop something to make life easier for us, if we relax and wait a moment, often they will stop on their own accord. Be in the feeling space you wish your home would ring with and watch it unfold around you.

Children live in the moment.

Their focus is on the now.

It is the reason they can be so within their joy that they skip down the street, and why it feels so off to them when they have to wait. With their unwavering focus on their Now they don't hesitate in feeling good, they are aware and alert to every experience they can have.

Provided we don't convince them to hesitate under the illusion of fear and stress.

That tightening feeling when we worry about the opinions of others or the future is an indicator of spirit.

We can not be connected when we worry so we need to make a shift.

You are doing your best, you are exactly where you need to be at this moment, and you are doing exceptionally well. Others may not understand you, and you may not know what's to come, but your *power* is in your moment.

Make it one of wellbeing.

*We teach our children kindness*

*by being kind,*

*forgiveness*

*by forgiving,*

*happiness*

*by being happy,*

*love*

*by loving*

*and wellbeing*

*by trusting that all is indeed well.*

Although we might try to demand to be understood, listened to, and in control of our family experiences, it all falls away when we focus on connection. Connection to our true selves, and everything we really are, releases the resistance that forcing things create within us.

Therefore, if we take a moment to breathe, connect and love, our words will be heard, our life will flow and control won't be needed.

If our children experience conflict we encourage them to act in peace, to rise above the disagreement and be true to who they are, yet this tool is only truly given through our own example.

In order to be the aware parent we wish to be, we must be conscious of our own reactions, and be the example of someone who acts from connection, rather than just ask our children to act from source instead.

Life is a process of bliss and contrast.

When we experience something that causes us pain or upset we learn what we don't want. We then can focus on it, and live the upset *or* shift to feeling for the solution.

Like attracts like and the more we focus on the solution the quicker the pain will be resolved. This is the same for our children and why the art of distraction is one of the greatest gifts we can offer them.

There doesn't need to be a plan.

We don't need to know who our children will become, or what they will do when they grow up. We don't need to fill our heads with what will happen next year, next fall or next week. Our focus should always be to create happy moments and to appreciate the life in front of us.

Enjoy each smile, each laugh and childhood sparkle, allowing life to create more of the same.

Children like to explore feeling off.

This usually appears with fear and watching scary movies or telling scary stories. This is the perfect opportunity to introduce the tool of shifting focus, especially before sleep. Help them find things to appreciate, and focusing on pretty stories and thoughts. Offer them the tools of finding ways of feeling good, and then the contrast they've explored will serve them well.

Habits are formed through life and it's not just biting nails or eating chocolate.

It is easy to form habits in the way we think, either about our children, the world, our bodies or ourselves. If a negative thought pops in sometimes it can just be the result of a habitual progression of thinking. Therefore, we need to look at our negative trains of thoughts, and create good habits of thinking only on the good.

Expect the unexpected, but always with the best possible outcome.

Moments of joy come in all shapes and sizes and we hold them back when we try to control or define them. From a bus ride with our children, to a happy cuddle at bedtime, look for the chances to bring you the feeling you are constantly craving.

We all wish for relief and joy. It can come in so many ways, so be the change you wish to see in your life.

No matter how many books you read, how many forums you join, or how many family members offer advice, you have the ultimate re*Source* at your finger tips.

Within yourself lies the answers to every question. Follow your instincts, find the peace within to let your heart shine and know your own truth.

For by being true to yourself you offer your child everything you are and everything they came here to experience.

when things are a struggle and feeling off,
take a step back and refocus.

Perhaps there's a small change or an easier
option to take. Often, when you reassess
the matter and relax into wellbeing, an
easier solution will appear and all things
will flow again. It's the difference between
being stressed and smiling through the day
and that is a shift worth working for.

A group of people can experience the same event, but come out of it with different perspectives.

This goes for a family too. If a parent or a child has settled into a frustrated perspective, than even the most exciting experience will frustrate them. If they have established a joyful point of view, then they will always be able to find something to be joyful about. Set the example and BE the wellbeing and enjoy.

*Breathe* deeply, letting your stomach rise with the incoming breath.

Relax your muscles, letting them drop onto your bed as if floating on a cloud.

Appreciate all the wonderful things in your life and ease your way into wellbeing with a satisfying letting go.

These 3 steps can easily be passed on to a hyper child, and offers them the tools of a lifetime as a quick step towards connection.

Breathe

Life for all of us is a steady stream, which is full of wellbeing when its allowed to flow, but when we hold our children back, or attempt to control their experience, we build a dam up against that wellbeing.

Therefore, we must sense who our children are anew each day, learning their new perceptions, perspectives and how they've grown, allowing their streams to flow, and for us to go along for the ride.

It's exhilarating to see the world thru what our children perceive as they see it thru different eyes then our own.

By listening to our children's excitement and wonder over things in their lives, by taking part in their explorations, sharing their thrills and feeling their passion for discovery, amazement and bliss, we can see a world that would have gone un-noticed to us otherwise.

Co-creation at its best.

For each problem, there is a solution.

For every negative there is a positive.

Everything has its flip side, and it is
only by our focus that one side becomes
the stronger.
It sometimes may take a bit of
meandering around, but sooner or later we
find a focus that feels better and when we
practice it...
it creates better days.

Even though it's the hardest time, it's in their off moments that our children need to be treated for the true spirits they really are.

When they are connected they need no reminder, rather it is when they are acting least themselves that, when we hold on to their true essence, they will fill that space and connect again.

If we protect from fear it can turn to trying to control our child's experience rather than preventing injury.

Trying to control life to always have happy outcomes takes away our child's power of their own feeling space, their own instincts and feeling the contrast when something feels off to it feeling great. Feel good now, and trust that good outcomes will come, than protect from that place of love.

It's all good. Believe it or not, it really is.

Oh sure, life might sometimes seem like a rapids on a raft, sometimes everything kicks into high gear and you feel like you have to push, push, push to keep up.

Pushing against the current of our lives never gets us anywhere.

So, relax, lie back and let life carry you to the next space in life. Some things may feel off, some may feel good, and then there's always that in between, but focus on what is well, and feel the flow of life carry you along.

Can you imagine the feeling of having
*your voice always being heard,*
*your feelings listened to and respected,*
*your perspectives supported,*
*your opinions counted,*
*and your changes and growth understood and validated?*

Can you imagine the sense of freedom in all of that?
If this is a feeling we want for ourselves, then we can offer it for our children, and in giving it, reap the experience for ourselves as well.

There's a saying somewhere that life is like driving at night, with the headlights only show you a few feet infront of you, but by following that course you get where you want to go.

Trust your Now. Focus on the positive, and revel in the bad, as it too is part of the journey.

Every pot hole makes us appreciate the newly paved road all the more.

we all use our imaginations all the time. Anytime we speculate on future events, or replay the past in our minds, we call forth the power of the imagination. Therefore why not harness that power to create anew? Why not encourage our children to do the same? By imagining the life we want, or how we want our parenting experience to be, we create the space for it to come.

Therefore give yourself the space to daydream.

Our own personal experience as an example is one of the best parenting tools we can offer our children.

Not only how we speak and act, but how we grow, learn, use our intuition, express how we feel, follow indicators, focus on the positive and live in the moment.

It offers our children insight and a natural default for happy living in the state of wellbeing.

*That morning tea or coffee,*
*the first dive into water on a hot day,*
*biting into our favorite treat,*
*the smell of our children's hair,*
*their smile,*
*their laugh*
*their play.*

*There's so many things to appreciate and*
*reconnect us to life Source, if we chose to become*
*aware to them.*

*Breathe, love, laugh and thrive*

Each moment offers an opportunity to reach for a better feeling thought.

For our babies, this can be done with the use of other activities, then as they get older we can help shift focus to positive things around them, and then, bringing their awareness to find better feeling thoughts themselves.

This is the root of The Art of Distraction, which is truly an art. To look, in each moment, for better feeling options.

It's so easy to find excuses for not feeling good.
We blame the *weather, money,* even our own *children's behaviour* as things which, since we can't control them, can make us feel bad.

However, when we step away from the problem and shift focus onto feeling good, just thru thinking different thoughts, the solution suddenly appears anyway and the problem disappears.

Feel Good first, and resolve later.
It's a bit of a short cut to a happy day.

If we act from the awareness of how we
feel and how that feeling indicates
whether we are connected to our own
spirits or not, then we can have a deeper
understanding of ourselves
and of our children.
With this knowledge, we can work
moment to moment to feel better and get
connected to our source, as well as sense
how our children are feeling, and
encourage them to jive again.

Let your shoulders drop, breathe deep and
relax.

Let wellbeing become your perspective
and trust that everything is going just as it
should.
There are no *"have to's"*, no *"must have's"*.

We are all experiencing exactly what we
should be in this moment, to grow, to
expand and to get to the new place of
satisfying joy.
This is true for our world, our children
and for ourselves.

Breathe, trust, appreciate and love.

Everyone has off days,
including our children.
We may not always see it in a fit of
passion, sometimes it's just a steady run of
things going wrong for them.

As a parent we can let them work their
way thru it alone or, *as if offering them a hand
up out of a hole in the ground*, offer them
opportunities to laugh,
to see the bright side,
to distract,
to shift focus,
thereby helping them shift their point of
attraction.

As a parent we have so many opportunities to stop and "be".

From nursing our babies, car rides with our children, mealtimes, bedtimes, they all give a chance to stop, connect and enjoy.

Sometimes our minds chatter thru these moments, putting the focus on the future. But when we seize them, life becomes sweeter. We can tap into all we truly are, breathe and BE!

The words we use for to our children set the tone of how they view themselves.

Imagine the difference to being called *"Darling"* or *"Special"* compared to the feeling of *"Trouble"* or *"Silly"*.

Even our children overhearing us talking about them to others in this way becomes a deciding factor to how our children feel about themselves as they grow.

Therefore, we should always remember to only say things about them, that we would want to have said about ourselves.

When we want something we often put so
much attention on the "want" that it is all
we see.
It is only by trusting that on some level
our desires have been met
and then to relax,
knowing it will come in perfect timing,
that we can enjoy our Now and allow the
desire to flow in.

To teach this to our children, even
through example, prevents the
disconnected behaviour of someone who
can't have what they want.

Before they came to us our children were
pure, positive beings.
They chose to come to us not because
they had something to fix or something to
learn, but only for the experience of life,
and to have what we can offer as the
launching place for it.

*What a thing to appreciate.*

Love, love, love and breathe.

Everything is perfect
and when we relax into the knowledge of
this, little wrinkles in the road seem to
smooth out seamlessly.

There is often something that is a worry
or rubs us the wrong way, but when we
direct our focus away from it, even for a
little, there's always new perspective.

Laugh, breathe and relax.
You are doing exceptionally well.

Emotions such as *irritation, frustration, anxiety* or *upset* are indicators of not acting from a connected place, for both ourselves and our children.

By being aware of how we feel,
we can see the red light flashing
and rather than pretending it's not there
(or blaming our little ones for it being
there in the first place)
and driving thru it,
we can stop, focus on something that
feels better, reconnect, and continue.

**Don't let your parenthood define you,
let you define your parenthood.**

Be everything you are now,
from the launching place of
where you have been
and allow yourself the chance to grow
and change in each coming day.

Trust yourself, and by focusing on the
positive and feeling good, let everything
you are flow in.

words are overrated.

Even from conception, we all
comprehend from interpreting energy.
Babies sense what we feel and in turn they
communicate to us by intention.
By taking a moment to be still and relax in
Who We Really Are, we sense how they
feel and enter a place where
words aren't needed.

Our children can then feel secure
knowing they are understood at their
deepest level.

Action based living, and focusing on the
"*doing*" part of our lives, can prevent us
from seeing the beauty of the living
moment in front of us.

When we focus on "*being*"
rather than "*doing*",
we live each moment and the action
required from us come organically out of
the situation, rather than us logically
thinking our way through it.

when we're stressed, our children get stressed, then we get stressed more, they do more... round and round she goes.

It's important to remember that while we have a past knowledge of changes and life's movements, for a child NOW is their everything.
Change and stress can rock a child to their core, so it's our understanding of how they feel, and providing security in the little things, that makes a difference.

From the very beginning, our children are so clear on whether they are connected to their source or not.

A connected child laughs, smiles, and all things go well for them, a disconnected child cries over everything, falls over everything and basically falls apart.

As an aware parent we can understand "off" days. Therefore, there's no reason to be mad. Simply hug them, love them, make them smile and Breathe deeply.

To commit to feeling good anyway is a
powerful stance for a parent.
It is chose our focus about how we feel,
rather than be a vibrational sponge and
take on whatever feelings come our way.

Not only does this create how our days
go, but it helps our children chose
whether they will let others control how
they feel, or direct it themselves.

Whether we Act or React is a question for
all of us.

We feel we should teach our children about spiritual truths forgetting that they understand them already.

They are closer to Spirit where they are in life, but haven't the reference system to verbalize it yet. They just know the joy of connection and the pain of disconnection.

Therefore as a parent, we don't have to <u>teach</u> them what they already feel, just help them connect more often than not, so the offness doesn't become a habit.

Some people hear
*"feel Good"*
as
*"Do whatever you want."*

Living by our own spiritual awareness
doesn't mean we try to control life to
make us feel better, rather it is about
feeling better through our thoughts,
through whatever comes our way,
getting connected and letting life flow in.

True connection would never allow
hurting, criticizing, or controlling others to
feel Truly Good as it goes against our own
spiritual truth.

**Now** isn't this week, this day,
or in 5 minutes.
**Now** is this very moment in time and it is
such a powerful thing.

If we take that **Now** and shift focus to
appreciating our toddlers,
holding our sleeping baby a little longer,
connecting with our unborn,
listening to our children
and raise how we feel to a place of loving
radiance,
our days improve and we feel more
ourselves as we let the wellbeing flow in.

Love is a powerful source
(I refuse to call it a *force*, as it flows and
can never be forced).

When we appreciate someone or
something we love and let that feeling
drop to our core being, we can feel the
emotional, spiritual and physical benefits
as our heart swells and our lungs expand
in the "aha" moment of it.

When we always reach for that state, and
live in it, we never have cause to expect
unhappy outcomes.

It's so inspiring to take a minute and try to see life thru the eyes of our children. Imagine how things look to them, get a sense of what inspires them, thrills them, frustrates them.

Rather than logically telling ourselves what our children are like, by imagining life through their eyes we can tap into the essence of Who They Really Are and emotionally feel our way to what they are experiencing and what they need.

Being spiritually aware means that even in our off moments we can be aware that under everything there is a spring of wellbeing that flows for us if we just let it.

It is our own perspective that makes the "*off*", all it takes is to breathe, relax and shift focus to what flows for us, to what feels good, and then life is beautiful again.

Awareness is knowing whether we are "off" or connected, and working to feel better.

Do you ever let people's stories fill your head and go round like a movie, only to then give an emotional reaction to it?

It is a distraction, but not a creative one, for it distracts us from our own moment, our child's moments, and our time together. It fills us with a feeling space that isn't our own, and clouds a day, leaving us giving half focused nods to our children, rather than a present version of who we are.

90% of the time when we could react to our children's behaviour in a disconnected way, it's when they are having fun or looking into a situation in order to have fun, or, having gotten carried away in fun, done something that is either messy or dangerous.

If we react, we then become the "no-fun" one. Whereas if we ACT, and bring more fun into the space, life and exploration will continue, but the offness won't.

Every child will occasionally speak sharply, throw a tantrum, or not listen and it doesn't make them any less perfect.

If each of us didn't try out things that created a negative feeling inside of us we would never know how wonderfully relieving it feels to feel good.

Rather than seeing negative actions as problems, we as parents can understand that they build awareness and appreciate their use.

It's so easy for us all to get caught up in the how's and why's.

Our children do it to, especially when their moment feels off to them, action seems like the best choice in order to change how life is going.

However, if we can relax into wellbeing, and return to the natural state of knowing that Source is better at planning than we are, we and our children can learn to simply allow the goodness to flow in.

when we feel anger in a specific situation it doesn't stay bound to that one element of life. Rather it spreads over every element, like a black cloud.

Positive emotion is the same, and when we chose to find a positive perspective in a single moment, that shift takes place in all elements of our day.

In this way we truly create our reality, as by what we put focus on spreads like a ***spiritual golden touch.***

Often the easiest option is to blame others, including our children, for the offness of a moment.

However, Life is about perspective.

Our beliefs will always be backed up by life around us.

Therefore when we focus on the positive elements of our families, more proof of that will appear in the day.

When we blame others for feeling *off*, we simply are seeing them in the negative view that made us off in the first place.

Sometimes what appears to be a "Have to do" list, upon second glance turns out to be a "Have to keep busy" list.

It's a delicate balance, but we can form a habit of keeping busy, that we never have time to enjoy life and play.

Take a walk and talk to your children, play, listen to their stories and then set time aside to do that "Have to" list, rather than keeping busy, and then setting time aside to play.

Have you ever noticed that when you smile at someone, they usually smile back?

We truly do get what we give.

However, it can also work the other way, and if we are simply reacting to others, when they act in a negative way, they will get  the same back from us.

Like attracts like, feelings build upon each other. So therefore, we should ask ourselves the question-

what feeling are we sending out, and do we want to get it back?

It is important to remind ourselves that our children are themselves.

They are just like us.

They *observe*,

*create*,

*laugh*,

*decide*,

*like*, *dislike*,

*love* and *live*.

At no point in time are they less than us, at no point do we have a right to control them.


**We are all one, on different parts of different paths of the same road.**

we get what we push against every time.

Therefore, rather than putting attention on how we don't want our children to grow up too fast, or don't want them to get mixed up with the wrong people, we can switch from reacting with fear and respond with the perspective of love.

By putting attention on what we do want and seeing each small piece of evidence to support it in our children daily we open up the gate ways for everything to flow in.

Provided all went well, one of the most blissful moments we can ever have is just after the birth of a child.

With pregnancy behind us and in no hurry to start thinking of future we can drift into the perfection of being with the new love in our life, counting their toes, kissing their hair and loving each breath.

We should try to find similar moments daily- with no past, no future just delicious appreciation in the moment.

we all have spoken when we shouldn't, acted goofier than the moment was right for, spoken sharper than we wished. **Often, we have all been less than socially perfect.**

Therefore, rather than trying to control every move of our child's behaviour, we can tell them how much we relate, what we learnt from it, and validate their own feelings about whatever they've done and allow them to form their own opinions for the future.

we are constantly discerning in life.

In each moment, we are deciding which road to take, which way feels better, which choice "makes sense."

In many ways, this is how we state Who We really Are.

However, often we can get bogged down in choices and we spin about finding the best solution. Relax in it all. Appreciate yourself into a state of wellbeing and connect first. Then that truest you will make the truest choice.

Sleep is a state of total connection.

How we sleep, and dream, are indicators to the feeling space we have in the day and we will often wake up in the same feeling space we went to sleep with.

Therefore, we can create a better day by appreciating ourselves to sleep, and drifting off to a blissful state.

What a empowering tool to give our children, whose dreams can provide us with indications of how they are feeling.

when we are aware of Who We Really Are
and connect to that truest part of
ourselves we tap into our instinctual gut
feeling in every moment.

We can't figure out instincts, we can't
decide what they will be in the future and
we have to allow them to change in each
circumstance. Therefore, by being
connected, by feeling good and true to
ourselves we instinctually sense which step
to take next at each given moment.

As parents one of the biggest challenges we face is *focus*.

It seems we train ourselves to juggle numerous balls at one time, from listening to everyone at once, answering the phone and trying to change a baby.

A young child doesn't scatter their thoughts, but focuses on something of interest, even if it's a bug on the sidewalk for a moment.

To focus as they do keeps our vibration pure and our attraction point clear.

Appreciate the gift of play.

In a moment of creative play, a child can learn to change how they feel, shift gears and distract themselves towards happier outcomes. By encouraging our children to find their inner toolbox of their imagination, by setting them up with a game or craft, rather than getting frustrated by the haranguing chorus of "I'm bored", we offer them more than amusement, we offer them tools for life.

Become the observer of your own life.

When we take the time to sit back and look at our own lives and households as if watching a movie we can release our own reaction state and sink back into a place of wellbeing. We can then tell a better story about what we see, changing perspectives about what we've witnessed and understand our children's viewpoints and those of others around us.

Breathe, relax and observe.

Our children grow and expand and with that what they need and want change too.

When we trust our own connection and listen to our children on the deepest of levels we can feel what changes need to be made and a shift will occur naturally.

However, when their surroundings change before they feel ready to, we can provide them with the security of play, laughter and fun which makes all transitions connected ones.

Families are like tapestries, a work of art.

They start with a vision, but it is the moment by moment that create the fabric of our lives. We never know how each thread will pull together, and often we think we've made mistakes, but if we hold true to what we dream the feeling of our home will ring with, as the fabric develops so too will the art within.

Soon we will see, it's going even better than envisioned.

when a child is scared, we can help them find cause to smile,

when they are sad we can give them opportunity to laugh.

When the feeling space of the home is aggravated we can create a window to shift it to harmonious.

As parents, we are only in charge of our own feeling spaces, but we can always create the opportunity for our children to shift with us, reminding them that we can pick which side of emotion to resonate on.

Sometimes its our perception of how our children are behaving rather than their behaviour itself that throws us off.

When we are connected, their playing makes us smile while when we are stressed and disconnected the same scenario can grate on our nerves.

It doesn't mean we can't ask for calm. Rather we can explain to them how we are feeling and stop blaming them for our discomfort, reminding ourselves of Who they Are.

It's often just about focus, about listening to our children with our hearts as well as ears, which can help them connect again.

To offer them ourselves throughout the day, without letting other thoughts take the forefront, not only empowers and validates them to be themselves, it also empowers us.

When we treat people the way we wish to be treated, it always feels good. The bonus is, we always get what we give.

No matter what negative experiences we have; *be it in a traumatic birthing experience, sickness, poverty,* connection can always be found when we remember that it is the bad times that form life.

In them we chose what we like and what we don't, we define who we are and who we want to be. We can choose to focus on the bad and muddle around in it, or see it for what creates and live the newer version of ourselves.

Do you like to be listened to?

*So do our children.*

Do you like it when a plan you have made goes smoothly?

*So do they.*

Do you like to feel free to think whatever you wish?

*Our children do too.*

Children are no different than us except they have a different perspective, a newer vantage point and less experience being here.

We do not control or own them; we're just here to give them a good start on the journey of life.

A child doesn't need to be forced to do what's "right". We don't have to demand them to be "good". Like every being on this planet at their core, our children are pure, positive, beings.

Being kind, considerate, helpful, thoughtful and radiate makes them feel wonderful and being anything less, for all of us, feels awful.

If we offer them tools to truly feel good and be true to themselves, than discipline will fade into the past like a bad memory.

Feeling sick or tired, although signs of physical problems, are routed in a deeper level. When we are disconnected from Who We Really Are we receive indicators of it in our physical bodies.

Therefore, when our children suffer we can help them by making them laugh and distracting them from their discomfort. Tiredness can be overcome by focusing on appreciation and the wellbeing in our lives just before going to sleep.

For both ourselves and our children it is vital to find that inner spark, that flow of energy that makes us dance and laugh.

Sometimes we all hit a rut, a feeling space that becomes a habit and is hard to shake. But with a bit of distraction, a bit of creative activity, a new game, even a walk outside, life can flow again and connection for our children will always be indicated with a certain sparkle in their eyes.

when we worry we imagine the worst.

When we fight, we imagine what we could have said.

When we're hurt we imagine what we'd like to do.

Children serve dolls air as food, and hear figurines talk. They know how to use their imaginations to have fun, feel better and create positive experiences.

We all need to be as children, and use our imaginations to feel the wellbeing that is ever flowing around us.

Be careful what you complain about.

Of course there are always things that bother us every now and then, but it's important to keep them in their place.

When we feel the need to complain we should acknowledge it, know what it is we're complaining about, offer it up and let it go. Otherwise, if we keep repeating it over and over, it becomes our perspective and its all we can see.

Soon we'd complain about everything.

It isn't supposed to be hard to feel good. Rather if things feel *off*, than they are *off* and a shift needs to occur.

Distract yourself from your current routine, find a reason to laugh, play with your children, and see the world through their eyes.

Suddenly sunlight will pour through the crack in the wall, and wellbeing will flow and it will feel so wonderful to be connected to Who You Really Are once again.

Everything that has gone before has brought us to the place and perspective of where we stand today.

With it behind us, we can offer our children and all of those around us a fuller version of us.

We are ever evolving beings.

As we've experienced we've made new self defining decisions from each new vantage point. Therefore, start the day afresh, and be exactly who you've always dreamed you could be.

when a problem comes to our attention
we have two options, we can focus on it,
struggle with it, and attempt to wrestle it
to the ground, or we can acknowledge it,
focus on how we wish it would be and
then allow the solution to flow in.

When we focus on a problem that is all we
can see.

When we focus on a solution, it will come
in the most extraordinary way and will
always make life better than before.

when things are *off* for our children,

they let us know.

However, if we jump into the problem too, we can't offer any alternative. Our children create their own feeling spaces and we can't fix anything by band-aiding the situation.

Rather, offer distraction, point out things to appreciate, hug them, love them, see them for the best they are, and with that image let them feel their way better, one step at a time.

Our children grow and expand and, with that, what they need and want change too.

. When we trust our own connection and listen to our children on the deepest of levels we can feel what changes need to be made and a shift will occur naturally.

Also, when their surroundings change before they feel ready to, we can provide them with the security of play, laughter and fun which makes all transitions connected ones.

Our children want and want… constantly eager for what the new will bring.

By encouraging appreciation for the now and reminding them of instances where they have gotten what they wanted once they had let it go and forgotten about it, allows them to not be disconnected because they can't see their desires in front of them.

Learning to allow life to flow in and trusting in wellbeing is a gift to last a lifetime.

Be prepared for opportunity to knock, but never in the way you expect.

When you want something, even something small like an exchange with your children, a moment of peace, a break from the everyday, Source has infinite ways of setting it up, but we can be so busy in focusing on not having it, we pass it by.

Know all is well and exactly as it should be and suddenly, the perfect chance for what you want will appear.

As nice as it feels to protect our children from outside influences, from the wrong crowd, or the wrong scenario, nothing feels more connected as watching them keep true to themselves in that which we try to protect them from.

By empowering them to be everything they are and stay true to that, we offer them the finest protection. It is one made of love and trust, rather than out of fear and lack of understanding.

A child makes a plan on what they feel will make them happy, but if it feels *off* to us we intervene. If we distract them onto something that will equal the joy they were reaching for, they get the same result and stay connected.

So too does the universe provide for us. We may think we know how life should go, but by focusing on joy in the now, we allow for that joy to flow towards us in ways we couldn't even imagine.

when there's a moment in the day where everything stops and you have time to do that bit of extra cleaning, or check email, or watch tv- STOP.

Give yourself some time before jumping into yet another activity. Take that moment, enjoy the stillness, breathe deeply and find yourself somewhere in the open, expansive space you've created.

Release yourself to the Now moment and then return to what you were going to do.

As much as it feels like control is the easiest answer sometimes, when we take the moment to connect we find the last thing we want from our children is compliancy.

Rather, when we connect with our source and our children we have the opportunity to co-create with them, letting their instincts have as great as value as our own, and offering them the tools to be themselves while not stamping on others.

what grounds you and puts you in a place of connection?

Personal keys to wellbeing can change time to time, but we all have some reliable constants to fall back on into a place of awareness. Therefore, breathe, relax, focus and love. feel the wellbeing of the moment. It is a wondrous thing to stop within our busy days, connect and know that all is indeed well and perfectly balanced.

Perhaps one of the greatest thing we can learn from our children is their ability to move forward, always expanding to the new adventure. They are curious of the new and eager to explore new ground, and often as parents we want to suppress it in the name of being safe.

By being aware of the exploration, and guiding it safely, we can jump on board our child's natural craving, and avoid becoming stagnant ourselves.

Knowing that negative emotion is an indicator of disconnect in our children gives a parent a powerful tool, as rather than react to our child's behaviour we can offer assistance to ease their discomfort and help them find connection again.

As they get older, they can use this tool themselves and reach for connection rather than struggle through what they are feeling.

Patience isn't something we gain or something we achieve, it isn't something to work towards.
Rather patience is a state of being we can enter whenever we wish.

To be patient is to step aside from our current reality, breathe, relax and let wellbeing flow over us. To be patient is to choose to not act or react, but to stand peacefully suspended in time, until the right action appears.

Our children's behaviour is a reaction to how they feel and what they think, but that isn't always something they can put in words.

But tapping in to their true selves with open hearts and minds and seeing past what they present to us at the moment, we can feel what they are going through and deal with it on a deeper level, lifting them out of where they are and helping them find a better feeling place.

We experience this world through our senses and in doing so form opinions, perspectives, and preferences.

Our children do this from before birth, and are fascinated by all of their sensory reality, which we often take for granted.

But by *hearing*, *smelling*, *seeing*, *tasting* and *feeling* intently, we can tap into a deeper sense of living and appreciate so much more.

whoever we perceive our children to be,
and how we expect them to act, we will
always find evidence to support the belief.

That goes for everything in life, we might
not get what we expect in the exact detail,
but we will always have the feeling place
matched.
Therefore, when we see the best in our
children, we offer the space for them to
be it, and when we see the best in life we
offer the space for it to flow in.

Parenting is a wonderful circle.

By taking care of our own thoughts and feeling place, we create a better place for our children to thrive in and provide them with tools to create a beautiful life for themselves offered by example, and we live happy days ourselves.

The alternative is to attempt to offer our children happy lives from an unhappy source, which is impossible.

Who we are is, in the long run, all we have to offer them.

All in good time. Everything truly has its perfect time and there's no need to push.

From a child's first step or word, potty training, weaning or important "discussions" we're told need to be given, offer them all up to Source, asking for the perfect moment and then allow that moment to appear.

Seize it, and all will flow. Your child and you have unique timing that will create the perfect experience.

Find peace in your present moment.

Even if children won't sleep, or you can't finish something you've started, if everything seems to be going wrong and it all seems overwhelming, simply stop and find peace.

By focusing on your moment and creating a smile in it, things will fall into place. By pushing against the moment and focusing on the next, things will continue to build momentum.

we are often quick to judge or criticize new people or situations that come into our children's lives.

When we criticize we push the *deconnection* button.

Rather if we act from love we stay connected and then we can follow our instincts which lead us to situations and people that our children will blossom with. We will be inspired with how to talk to our children openly and we will see people on a deeper level.

Oh, to live in the moment the way a young child does!

Even though one moment will be disconnected, a little one can shift focus quickly, connect, laugh, and jive without looking back, without questioning themselves, or wondering how it looks to others.

Aren't we lucky to live with such inspiring sources of pure joy?

What a life it would be if we could all achieve that freedom and empower our children to keep it with them always.

Our thoughts can be used to transform our feeling state, but if we focus on our thoughts, they tend to race and skip about.

This goes for children as well, and we can help them to try and find time for a

"quiet head".

When we find peace in our thoughts we allow how we feel to flow forth, and with a bit of help from the imagination, or focus on breath and feeling joy, we will find we think and feel so much better.

You are exactly where you are suppose to be in this moment.

Everything is perfect.

For in each *off* moment, you define yourself, you make a choice of what you want and what you don't.

Life is about the journey, with all it's bumps in the road. Its about moving to the next point of ease and flow, not hanging around the bump.

Focus on all that goes well, shift to what feels good.

After all, the journey always continues.

For more information about
Spiritually Aware Parenting and
Christina Fletcher's work, please visit
www.spirituallyawareparenting.com

or join the ever growing community at
www.facebook.com/whotheyreallyare
for more inspiring *Moments*.

www.ingramcontent.com/pod-product-compliance
Lightning Source LLC
Chambersburg PA
CBHW060928040426
42445CB00011B/848